ILLUSTRATION:
WHAT'S THE
POINT?

ILLUSTRATION:
WHAT'S THE
POINT?

MOUNI FEDDAG

ilex

AN HACHETTE UK COMPANY
WWW.HACHETTE.CO.UK

FIRST PUBLISHED IN GREAT BRITAIN IN 2017 BY
ILEX, A DIVISION OF OCTOPUS PUBLISHING GROUP LTD
OCTOPUS PUBLISHING GROUP,
CARMELITE HOUSE,
50 VICTORIA EMBANKMENT,
LONDON, EC4Y ODZ

PUBLISHER: ROLY ALLEN
EDITORIAL DIRECTOR: ZARA LARCOMBE
MANAGING SPECIALIST EDITOR: FRANK GALLAUGHER
EDITOR: RACHEL SILVERLIGHT
ART DIRECTOR: JULIE WEIR
ARTWORKER: GINNY ZEAL
PRODUCTION CONTROLLER: MESKEREM BERHANE

ISBN   978-1-78157-391-4

A CIP CATALOGUE RECORD FOR THIS BOOK
IS AVAILABLE FROM THE BRITISH LIBRARY.

PRINTED AND BOUND IN CHINA.

10 9 8 7 6 5 4 3 2 1

ILLUSTRATION IS GOOD FOR

BRINGING PEOPLE CLOSER TO THINGS

IT DOES THIS BY:

ATTRACTING

ENGAGING

DELIGHTING

INFORMING

CONTEXTUALISING

SHOWING

SHIFTING

SOOTHING

SYMPATHISING

STAYING

ILLUSTRATION BRINGS PEOPLE
CLOSER TO THINGS BY

ATTRACTING

(WHAT WE NOTICE IS CLOSER TO US)

BEING TRICKED OR DISAPPOINTED
IS UNPLEASANT.

BUT IF NO ONE NOTICES A GOOD THING,
YOU MAY AS WELL HAVE LEFT IT.

BEAUTIFUL THINGS CAN ATTRACT ATTENTION IN A
NOBLE AND EFFECTIVE WAY.

ALL GOOD THINGS CAN BE MISUSED.

NOTHING IS IN ITSELF GOOD OR BAD — IT ALL
DEPENDS ON HOW IT'S PUT INTO PRACTICE.

ATTRACTION IS JUST DISTRACTION THAT YOU ENJOY.

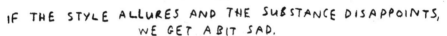

IF THE STYLE ALLURES AND THE SUBSTANCE DISAPPOINTS,
WE GET A BIT SAD.

BUT BEAUTIFUL PEOPLE AREN'T NECESSARILY ASSHOLES.

FEEL FREE TO JUDGE THINGS FROM THE OUTSIDE. WE DO IT ANYWAY.

THAT FORM/FUNCTION THING IS JUST THE CHICKEN/EGG QUESTION
FOR DESIGNERS WITH NOTHING BETTER TO TALK ABOUT.

'IF IT DOESN'T ROCK, IT'S USELESS.'
— CHARLOTTE ROCHE ACTOR/PRESENTER/AUTHOR

ILLUSTRATION BRINGS PEOPLE
CLOSER TO THINGS BY

ENGAGING

(WHAT WE OCCUPY OURSELVES WITH
IS CLOSER TO US)

MEANWHILE IN THE FINE ARTS...

MEANING LIES IN THE EYE OF THE BEHOLDER

← I SHOWED THIS 'MEANWHILE' PICTURE TO MY PROFESSOR IN CLASS. SHE SEEMED TO LIKE IT, AND I WAS HAPPY. THEN SHE SAID THAT YES, THAT'S HOW IT REALLY IS IN THE FINE ARTS - AND IT MIGHT LOOK STUPID, BUT IT ISN'T. WHAT I'D ACTUALLY WANTED TO SHOW WITH THE PICTURE WAS THE MYTHICAL IDEA THAT MANY PEOPLE SEEM TO HAVE ABOUT FINE ART, AND BY THE ABSURDITY OF THIS IMAGE, SHOW THAT IT CAN'T SERIOUSLY BE LIKE THAT. AS IF - 'DESIGN IS PROBLEM-SOLVING AND ART IS EXPRESSION'! WHAT DOES THAT MEAN?

MANY SAY THE OFFENBACH UNIVERSITY OF DESIGN IS FREER (IN A GOOD WAY) THAN THE DARMSTADT FORMER POLYTECHNIC. WHAT DOES THAT MEAN?

MY PROFESSOR PROBABLY SAID SOMETHING COMPLETELY DIFFERENT ANYWAY.

SOMETIMES WE UNDERSTAND ONE ANOTHER WITHOUT UNDERSTANDING ONE ANOTHER.

IN GERMAN, 'SICH (MIT JEMANDEN) VERSTEHEN' MEANS 'TO GET ALONG,' IN ENGLISH. THAT CAN TRANSLATE BACK AS 'WIR KRIEGEN'S HIN', WHICH IS MORE LIKE 'WE MANAGE.'

IF YOU COME UP WITH SOMETHING YOURSELF, YOU REMEMBER IT BETTER. THAT'S BEEN SCIENTIFICALLY PROVEN.

I SHOWED THIS TEXT TO MY PROFESSOR IN CLASS. SHE EXPLAINED TO ME AGAIN WHAT SHE'D MEANT WITH THE FINE ART THING, AND I FORGOT IT AGAIN. I JUST REMEMBER DECIDING AFTERWARDS THAT WE'D SAID THE OPPOSITE BUT MEANT THE SAME.

↖ THE LITTLE PICTURES ARE JUST DECORATION, DON'T WORRY.

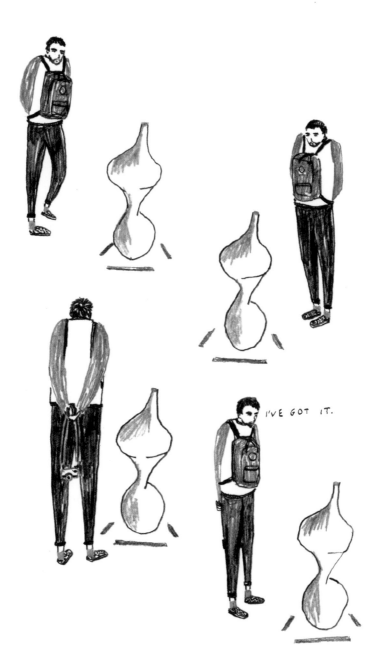

ILLUSTRATION BRINGS PEOPLE
CLOSER TO THINGS BY

DELIGHTING

(WHAT BRINGS US JOY IS CLOSER TO US)

PEOPLE ARE DYING IN AFRICA

- WITH THE TERM 'DECORATION' WE SEEM TO THINK OF SOMETHING LIKE PUTTING LIPSTICK ON A GORILLA.

- DECORATION IS ADDITIVE BY DEFINITION. SO TIDYING UP IS NOT DECORATING. BUT YOU NEED THINGS TO BE ABLE TO TIDY UP.

- WE MADE BEADS AND HEADDRESSES BEFORE WE MADE AXES. THERE ARE BIRDS THAT DECORATE THEIR NESTS — AND ARE REALLY PICKY ABOUT IT — SEEMINGLY FOR NO REASON BUT THEIR OWN PLEASURE (AND MAYBE MATING).

- WHEN ASKED IF HE DESIGNED FOR JOY OR FUNCTION, CHARLES EAMES REPLIED: 'WHOEVER SAID THAT JOY ISN'T FUNCTIONAL?'

- FUNCTION AND FORM USED TO BE ONE UNIFIED THING, WHEN OBJECTS WERE MADE BY ONE PERSON. IT WAS ONLY IN THE MID-19TH CENTURY THAT INDUSTRIAL PRODUCTION SEPARATED PLANNING FROM MAKING.

- WE TEND TO CONTRAST DECORATION WITH SIMPLICITY. SIMPLICITY HAS BEEN FASHIONABLE FOR SOME DECADES. AND THINGS LIKE CUSTOMER SERVICE AND TAX FORMS SHOULD BE SIMPLE. BUT DO WE WANT ONLY SIMPLE BUILDINGS, RELATIONSHIPS, CLOTHES, STORIES? IF EVERYTHING WAS SIMPLE, SIMPLICITY WOULDN'T MEAN MUCH ANYMORE.

- SOME SAY ILLUSTRATION SHOULDN'T BE ASSOCIATED WITH DECORATION, AND MANY SNEER AT ILLUSTRATIONS THAT ARE 'JUST DECORATIVE.' MANY WHO MAKE OR USE ILLUSTRATIONS TALK ABOUT HOW ILLUSTRATIONS 'SUPPORT' OR 'ENHANCE' A TEXT. ILLUSTRATIONS DON'T ENHANCE TEXTS, THEY TURN THEM INTO DIFFERENT TEXTS. DECORATIONS ALSO TRANSFORM.

- HOW IS DECORATION INVOLVED IN THESE ACTIVITIES: COOKING TRAINING, TALKING, SINGING, PLAYING, WRITING, ACTING, EATING, SITTING, DANCING, CLEANING...?

- SOME PEOPLE THINK THAT DECORATION MUST NECESSARILY BE SOMETHING USELESS. BUT DECORATION IS A FUNCTION IN ITSELF! MANY PEOPLE BELIEVE THAT, BY DEFINITION, DECORATION IS MEANINGLESS. BUT WHENEVER WE NOTICE SOMETHING, IT HAS A MEANING FOR US.

- MAYBE DECORATION IS AN ILLUSTRATION OF LOVE. (PAYING FOR LOVE CAN BE DODGY.)

- IF WE WERE ALL DOCTORS WITHOUT BORDERS WE'D END UP SAVING LIVES JUST FOR THE SAKE OF SAVING LIVES.

ILLUSTRATION BRINGS PEOPLE
CLOSER TO THINGS BY

INFORMING

(WHAT WE'RE TOLD IS CLOSER TO US)

GRÜNEBURGWEG

FÜRSTENBERGERSTRAßE

BREMER

HANSAALLEE

LEERBACHSTRAße

FELDBERGSTRAßE

WOLFGANGSTRAße

PARKSTRAße

AUF DER KÖRNERWIESE

BÖHMERSTRAße

FRIEDRICHSTRAßE

WIESENAU

ALTKÖNIGSTRAße

TELEMANNSTRAßE

GRÜNEBURGWEG

EMIL-CLAAR STRAßE

EPPSTEINER STRAßE

MYLIUSSTRAßE

KRONBERGER STRAße

ELSHEIMER STRAßE

STAUFENSTRAßE

GÄRTNE

FREIHERR-VOM-STEIN-STRAßE

REUTERWEG

IM TRUTZ FRANK

LEERBACHSTRAßE

LIEBIGSTRAße

WÖHLERSTRAße

UNTERLINDAU

OBERLINDAU

BOCKENHE

ARNDTSTRAße

LINDENSTRAße

LESSINGSTRAße

FEUERBACHSTRAße

BARCKHAUSTRAße

ULMENSTRAße

BOCKENHEIMER LANDSTRAße

KLEINE HOCHSTRAße

KAISERSTRAßE

KETTENHOFWEG

NIEDENAU

TAUNUSANLAGE

GUIOLLETTSTRAßE

NEUE MAINZER STRAße

NEUE ROTHOFSTRAße

KLEINE BOCKENHEIMER ST

GOETHESTRAßE

KLOBERSTRAße

LANDSTRAßE

JUNG

FÜRSTENBERGERSTRAßE
HAMMANNSTRAßE
FÜRSTENBERGERSTRAßE
OEDER WEG
GLAUBURGSTRAßE
WOLFSGANGSTRAßE
KEPLERSTRAßE
STALBURGSTRAßE
LERSNERSTRAßE
HEINESTRAßE
BORNWIESENWEG
SÖMMERRINGSTRAßE
ADLERFLYCHTSTRAßE
BAUSTRAßE
HERMANNSTRAßE
FICHARDSTRAßE
KOSEL
OBERWEG
HUMBOLDTSTR.
WEBERSTRAßE
ESCHERSHEIMER LANDSTRAßE
FINKENHOFSTRAßE
LEIMENRODE
MITTELWEG
EISERNE HAND
HEBELSTR.
SCHLEIDENSTRAßE
ECKENHEIMER LANDSTRAßE
QUERSTRAßE
JAHNSTRAßE
FELLNERSTRAßE
OEDER WEG
BLUMENSTRAßE
STERNSTRAßE
UNTERWEG
SCHEFFELSTRAßE
MERCATORSTRAßE
FRIEDBERGER LANDSTRAßE
BÄCKERWEG
MAUERWEG
ESCHENHEIMER ANLAGE
PETERSSTRAßE
BERGER STR
FRIEDBERGER ANLAGE
BLEICHSTRAßE
TAUBENSTRAßE
RAHMHOFSTRAßE
KATZENPFORTE
STIFTSTRAßE
STEPHANSTRAßE
BRÖNNERSTRAßE
SCHÄFERGASSE
FRIEDBERGER STR.
ALTE GASSE
SEILERSTRAßE
HEILIGKREUZGASSE
BÖRSENSTRAßE
BÖRSENPLATZ
SCHILLERSTRAßE
GROßE ESCHENHEIMER STRAßE
ZEIL
ZEIL

NOUS VOUS PROPOSONS

*MICHE KEBAB 4.00 €

*MICHE TAOUK 4.00 €

*MICHE KAFTA 4.00 €

*MAXI SAOUDA 4.00 €

*KEBAB 4.00 €

*GEANT KEBAB 4.50 €

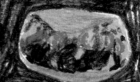
*SAOUDA 3.50 €

ILLUSTRATION BRINGS PEOPLE
CLOSER TO THINGS BY

CONTEXTUALISING

(WHAT WE UNDERSTAND IS CLOSER TO US)

ILLUSTRATION BRINGS PEOPLE
CLOSER TO THINGS BY

SHOWING

(WHAT WE CAN SEE IS CLOSER TO US)

NNING AIR NOTHING TOP PALM HEADSCARF GROUND
PLANT SKY BALLOON BLADE OF GRASS LEAF LOOKING GRASS
WOMAN MAN HORIZON HAT LEAF LEAF BELOW
MAN TREE MIDDLE HOT QUIET HAT
MMER LANDSCAPE FIELD FLOWERS LEAF BAG HEAD
COUPLE TUMMY WOMAN LEAF LEAF FOOTMAN HALF-LYING
RASS BLANKET BIKINI TOWEL LEAF PENCIL
READPENCIL LEGS WARMTH SCENE TROUSERS BLACK STRIPES
BELLY-BUTTON FOOT GRASS DECKSHOES DARK
PPLES FLOWERS GUY GIRL LYING
TOWEL TOWEL HOT TOWEL

GREEN GROUND LEAF FLOWER COMIC HAND BLOUSE
TOWEL PARK FLOWER FLOWER OPEN BUST
FOOT LEAF FLOWER FLOWER FLOWER GREEN GROUND GRASS
TOES TOES LEAF FLOWER FLOWER FLOWER
FOOT FOOT LEAF FLOWER FLOWER FLOWER
HIGH PENCIL LEAF FLOWER LEAF FRAME
WORDS THOUGHT BALLOON HOT-AIR-BALLOON
SPEECH TRENT REZNOR TRENT REZNOR
SPEECH-BUBBLE UNFINISHED EXPLANATION POINT AIR
SPOTS HEADSCARF BUBBLE OPINION BAND
FLORAL PATTERN NOTHING WHITE BACK MIRIAM WIND
LOOK EMPTY TURQUOISE DECORATION GLASSES NIN

SHOULDERS BEHIND NOTHING FEMALE NECK SHOULDER
BODY LANGUAGE
CURVE GESTURE LIGHT-BLUE
FRONT BLOUSE HAND
BREAST LIGHT-GREY ARM LONGSLEEVED BACKLINE
SPINE CORNER 2H POSTURE ARM
CROSS CUT-OFF

COLOURED-PENCIL PARK BIGGER FRAME
HAIRSTRAND EARTH EVERYTHING GREEN
ANTS LONG SPEECH-BUBBLE SHADE
OTHER ORDER POINT PATTERN LOVE
MOON BLACK FLOWERS GLASSES HAND BEANIE
SHADE EGG BAG STICK DECORATION
BOARD DUMB GAP AIR BORDER BLOUSE HAIR
NOSTRIL CHEEKS HAIR THIN SITTING D'OH
FLAT SMALL SOLES ANKLE GRASS GREASY
TOUCH LIGHT GREENS SNAKE IDIOT
FLAT ARROW QUESTION SHADE TWO PENCIL LYING WIDE
CHEST HEAVY MIDDLE UNIMPORTANT
BASKET FLAT CLOSE-UP FOOT SKIRT LITTLE-BUSH
CHUBBY INSECTS FLIP-FLOPS SMALL
UMMY FLOOR FLOWERS CUTE SHADE GRASS

END

'IT'S A DICTATORSHIP! ALL WORDS ARE PREFABRICATED, AND WE ONLY RECOGNISE THINGS WITH NAMES, ALTHOUGH WE PERCEIVE SO MUCH MORE.'

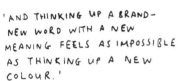

'AND THINKING UP A BRAND-NEW WORD WITH A NEW MEANING FEELS AS IMPOSSIBLE AS THINKING UP A NEW COLOUR.'

'AND WHEN WE NEED OR MAKE A NEW WORD, IT NEEDS TO BE DEFINABLE WITH OTHER WORDS!'

'WE'RE ALL DOOMED AND
NOTHING WILL EVER CHANGE!'

IT TOOK CENTURIES TO ESTABLISH OUR RELATIVELY
FEW COLOUR-NAMES. (ALTHOUGH WE COULD ALWAYS
DIFFERENTIATE BETWEEN MILLIONS OF COLOURS.)

TEXT AND PICTURE NEEDN'T
MEAN TEXT AND PICTURE.

PICTURES CAN MAKE TEXTS
AND TEXTS CAN MAKE PICTURES.

WORDS CAN MAKE
A PICTURE.

WORDS ARE ALSO
PICTURES.

PICTURES CAN
MAKE WORDS.

AND PICTURES CAN
MAKE WORDS.

TEXTS CAN MAKE
WORDS.

PICTURES AND WORDS
CAN MAKE TEXTS.

AN IMAGE CAN BE MADE OF
WORDS AND A TEXT CAN BE
MADE OF IMAGES.

BUT A WORD MUST
BE MADE OF LETTERS.

LETTERS ARE PICTURES.

ILLUSTRATION BRINGS PEOPLE
CLOSER TO THINGS BY

SHIFTING

(WHAT WE NOTICE AGAIN, DIFFERENTLY,
IS CLOSER TO US)

ILLUSTRATION BRINGS PEOPLE
CLOSER TO THINGS BY

SOOTHING

(WHAT'S ACCESSIBLE TO US IS CLOSER TO US)

WE FEEL SOMETHING PARTICULAR WHEN WE LOOK AT APPEALING PICTURES -
WE JUST DON'T HAVE A WORD FOR WHAT THAT FEELING IS. WE
DON'T HAVE WORDS FOR A LOT OF THINGS, AND THOSE THINGS ARE
NO LESS IMPORTANT. (I'M SCEPTICAL ABOUT THE WAY WE'VE
NAMED AND CLASSIFIED EMOTIONS. WE COULD ALWAYS SEE
MILLIONS OF COLOUR SHADES. WHEN WE HAVE A NAME FOR
SOMETHING, DO WE EXPERIENCE IT DIFFERENTLY?)

MAYBE COMFORT IS BETTER THAN ECSTASY. IT'S MORE SUSTAINABLE, ANYWAY.

VISION IS PROBABLY OUR FURTHEST-REACHING SENSE - WE SENSE THAT THE
OBJECTS WE CAN SEE ARE EXTERNAL AND SEPARATE TO US, AND DON'T EXPERIENCE
THEM INTERNALLY AS WE DO WHEN HEARING AND TOUCHING. BUT NOT ALWAYS.
MAYBE WE FEEL OBJECTS AND IMAGES THAT WE LOOK AT MORE WHEN THEY'VE
BEEN MADE WITH GREAT LOVE AND CARE.

THE THING WITH THE FIVE SENSES IS NONSENSE ANYWAY: MAYBE YOU CAN'T HEAR
A PICTURE BEFORE YOU'VE LOOKED AT IT, BUT NEITHER DO YOU EXPERIENCE SEEING
AND HEARING AND TASTING SEPARATELY. YOU JUST EXPERIENCE BEING. (ALTHOUGH,
ACTUALLY, I HAVE HEARD PICTURES BEFORE SEEING THEM, AND SEEN
MUSIC BEFORE HEARING IT.) ALL WE DO IS FEEL THINGS.

ANYWAY, NOW IT'S BEEN SCIENTIFICALLY PROVEN THAT LOOKING AT ART
IS GOOD FOR THE BRAIN. BEAUTIFUL PAINTINGS INCREASE THE
BLOODFLOW IN A SPECIFIC AREA OF THE BRAIN BY 10%, WHICH IS
THE EQUIVALENT OF WHAT HAPPENS WHEN YOU LOOK AT A LOVED
ONE. GOOGLE IT IF YOU DON'T BELIEVE ME. THE ARTICLE DOESN'T SAY
EXACTLY WHAT TYPE OF 'LOVED ONE' IS MEANT, OR IF THE PARTICIPANTS
WERE CONSCIOUS OF ANY OF THIS. BUT THE BLOODFLOW INCREASES BY
10%, WHICH PRESUMABLY MEANS IT GETS FASTER, AND ALL YOUR
ORGANS GET A BIT OF THE BLOOD, WHICH IS GOOD. OR MORE BLOOD
FLOWS THROUGH CERTAIN CHANNELS - THE ONES THAT GIVE YOU NICE
FEELINGS. I DON'T KNOW, BUT THEY MUST KNOW WHAT THEY'RE
TALKING ABOUT. THERE ARE SOME RATHER FUNNY STUDIES LIKE
THIS ONE. APPARENTLY IT SEEMS TO BE THAT WHEN ART MEETS
SCIENCE, IN THE SENSE OF SCIENCE RESEARCHING ART, EVERYTHING
KIND OF GETS STUCK.

ILLUSTRATION BRINGS PEOPLE
CLOSER TO THINGS BY

SYMPATHISING

(WHAT WE CAN RELATE TO IS CLOSER TO US)

GENERALLY, ILLUSTRATIONS ARE REPRODUCED PICTURES. SOME FIND IT STRANGE BY PRINCIPLE, EVEN DISHONEST, IF SOMETHING MECHANICALLY COPIED LOOKS HAND-DRAWN. BUT EVEN HELVETICA WAS MADE BY A FLAWED HUMAN LIKE YOU AND ME. AND SO WERE THE COMPUTERS AND PRINTERS.

I ALWAYS TELL MYSELF: 'STOP TALKING ABOUT YOURSELF! LISTEN TO THIS PERSON, ASK ABOUT THEIR LIFE!' OR: 'THAT'S HOW EVERYONE FEELS, YOU'RE NOTHING SPECIAL! SO STOP MOANING AND KEEP GOING!' IF THAT'S HOW EVERYONE FEELS, MAYBE WE SHOULD TALK ABOUT IT MORE. AND ACTUALLY, THE TEXTS I GET THE MOST OUT OF ARE COMPLETELY PER- SONAL. MAYBE I SHOULD JUST ADMIT THAT NONE OF YOU INTEREST ME AND ONLY EVER TALK ABOUT MYSELF. YOU MIGHT LIKE ME LESS FOR IT, BUT GET MORE OUT OF ME THAT WAY. MAYBE I'M WRONG AFTER ALL, MAYBE I'M NOT NICE AND QUIET AT ALL, BUT JUST SOME ARROGANT, UNSYMPATHETIC PERSON. MAYBE I'M A FAT FARMER'S WIFE OR A VILLAGE IDIOT. NO ONE KNOWS WHO THE VILLAGE IDIOT IS ANYMORE, BECAUSE WE'RE TAUGHT NOT TO ACT LIKE IDIOTS. MAYBE I WOULDN'T STUTTER AROUND SO AWFULLY IF I ALLOWED MYSELF TO ACT LIKE AN IDIOT. OK, THAT'S ENOUGH. I STILL NEED YOU TO TAKE ME A BIT SERIOUSLY.

ANYHOW, SURELY IT'S A GREAT THING THAT YOU CAN TAKE REPRODUCED PICTURES HOME WITH YOU, TO INTERACT WITH THEM AS YOU LIKE. PAINTINGS ARE GREAT TOO, BUT ULTI- MATELY EXHIBITIONS ARE WALKS WITH A CERTAIN NUMBER OF STOPS, WALKS WHERE YOU HAVE TO DRESS IN A CERTAIN WAY. THIS PICTURE, ON THE OTHER HAND, IS JUST FOR YOU. HONEST.

I'M ACTUALLY LEFT- HANDED (WHICH MAKES ME PRETTY SPECIAL) BUT I THOUGHT THE HAND FIT BETTER HERE ON THIS PAGE.

IN THE DARK

IN TEN MINUTES

RIGHT-HANDED

HALF-ASLEEP

BAD-MOODED

WALKING BACKWARDS

(I SHOULD PROBABLY TELL YOU THIS: THIS IDEA ISN'T MINE, IT'S ALAN FLETCHER'S. HE HAS A SIMILAR PAGE IN 'THE ART OF LOOKING SIDEWAYS'. THAT GAVE ME THIS IDEA - AND TOOK AWAY MY OWN. AND THESE WORDS ALSO AREN'T MINE, JUST THE ORDER AND THE HANDWRITING. AND EVEN THAT ONLY PARTIALLY.)

ILLUSTRATION BRINGS PEOPLE
CLOSER TO THINGS BY.

STAYING

(WHAT WE CAN REMEMBER
IS CLOSER TO US)

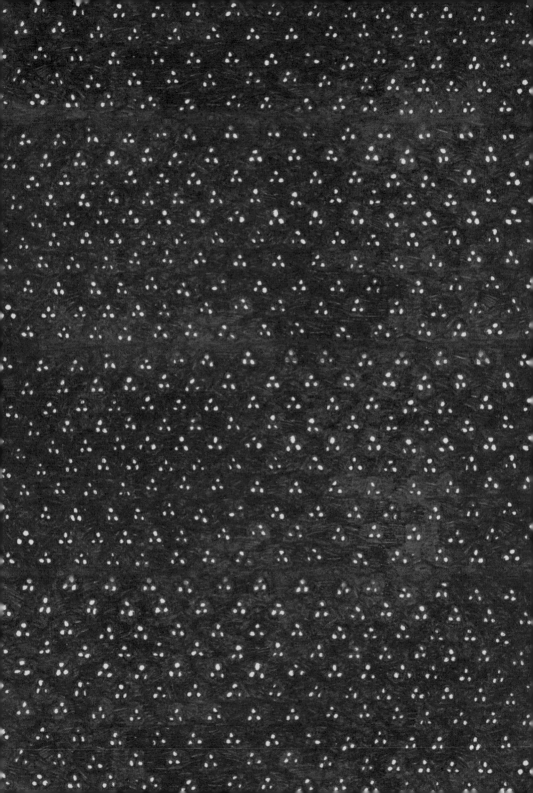

...CLING? CAN ONLY BE ANSWERED WITH ILLUSTRATION. WE LACK THE WORDS FOR MANY THINGS. WORDS ARE MORE THAN A TREE. A

...ESTUOUS SYSTEM. But not an inflexible one. WE FEEL SOMETHING PARTICULAR WHEN WE LOOK AT... WORDS COME FROM PICTURES

...THESE THINGS ARE NO LESS IMPORTANT. WORDS WERE MADE TO MAKE ... THERE ARE IDEAS

...ING PICTURES, WE JUST DON'T HAVE A WORD FOR IT. WORDS WERE ALREADY THERE.

...SE, PICTURES WERE MADE FOR BOOKKEEPING. WORDS ARE MORE THAN PICTURES, DO

...CAN ONLY BE EXPRESSED IN WORDS. YOU CAN ONLY BICKER ... AS SEPARATE WORDS

...EED THEM? WORDS ARE MORE THAN PICTURES. ... KNOWING IS DIFFERENT TO UNDERSTANDING

... words. ... PLAYING VIDEO GAMES GOES WITHOUT SAY.

...ls BUT LESS THAN PICTURES. THINGS AREN'T JUST

...ECT MEANS. A ... GOES WITHOUT SAYING. HOW I SEE

...WITH A ... ARE ONE AND THE SAME. ILL-

HAVE "HOW", "WHAT", "WHEN", "WHY", "WHO" AND "WHERE"

...'S WHY WE'RE A BIT CONFUSED. AND WHAT YOU DO WITH THEM.

...ation can help you understand things. ... INTO DIFFERENT TEXTS. THE

...EMEMBERING SITCOM CHARACTERS GOES WITHOUT SAYING.

THEY'RE ALSO HOW YOU GOT TO THEM AND WHAT YOU DO WITH THEM. ARE ONE AND THE SAME.

...I SEE. WHAT I SAY AND HOW I SAY IT ... MORE INTERESTING THAN THE INFORMATION

...TION DOESN'T ENHANCE TEXTS, IT TURNS THEM INTO DIFFERENT TEXTS.

...NTATION OF INFORMATION IS OFTEN MORE INTERESTING THAN THE INFORMATION. "LESS

...You can't gossip by yourself. QUANTITY IS A QUALITY IS A QUANTITY.

DRE. OR LESS." SOMETIMES REPETITION IS NECESSARY. DECORATION IS ALSO

...N'S NICHT ROCKT, IST ES FÜR'N ARSCH." WORDS/PICTURES WE ... A FUNCTION

THE WORDS AND THE WORDS OWN US. WORDS ARE BESTOWED WITH power

CANNOT FULFIL. WE DON'T THINK IN WORDS. Full stop. WORDS CAN

RESS VERY LITTLE. They can express a lot, but it's still very little. WORDS

...AREN'T ENOUGH. IT'S LIKE THAT SONG BY STING, "DE

SO HOW THEY FEEL. This isn't anything sentimental.

...HUNG. I can say what I like, you're going to earn decent money and I'll never leave my mum's

...oom. PHOTOGRAPHY REDUCES, DRAWING PRODUCES. MAYBE PHOTOS ARE BETTER

HOWING HOW THINGS LOOK, AND DRAWING'S FOR HOW THINGS FEEL.

YSE ILLUSTRATION SHOULD TAKE BACK SOME OF THE SPACE PHOTOGRAPHY HAS

FROM IT. REPRODUCING SOMETHING HAND-DRAWN IS NOT DISHONEST. "HAND-

N" AS A "STYLE" IS OKAY, IS LEGITIMATE. HANDMADE STUFF IS NICE BECAUSE IT'S

RELATABLE. RELATIVE OVER ABSOLUTE WE ONLY FIND GOOD/BEAUTIFUL

THINGS WHEN WE LOOK FOR THEM. BUT CRAPPY THINGS FIND US ALL THE TIME.

THERE'S NO WHITE OR BLACK, JUST GREY. Grey is nice. ALL GOOD THINGS CAN BE MISUSED

BIT WISHY-WASHY. THERE'S NOTHING ABSOLUTE, JUST RELATIVE. We can only

...see relative things. IF NOTHING'S ~~IMPORTANT~~ ABSOLUTE, NOTHING'S SENSE/THE POINT/Modern Think

INDEPENDENT. → Everything comes with a context. EVERYTHING IS ... "THE POINT" AND "SENSE" ARE SU

...IMPORTANT. CAN BE SUMMARIZED, LISTED, SORTED AND DEFINED ... LOOKS CRAP ANYWAY?" IS A VALID

EVERYDAY DIET. I COULD LIST THAT ILLUSTRATION JUST IS GOOD FOR BUT ... AT ALL. A NICE RIDE IS WORTH

...ange is no understanding without context. SIMPLICITY WOULDN'T EXIST WITHO ... WHERE YOU GET IS ALSO

COMMUNICATION IS TO MAKE TH ... Capitalism, advertising, bankers aren't ... NOT AS STRAIGHT AS I T

...is DIET AS A VARIED DIET. CONTEXT/FORM + CON ... SHOULD STOP DISLIKING ... WE CANNOT SEPARATE

WE SAY "LIKE". VERY ... it even more. ... There's no pure image o

ILLUSTRATE